Contents

We Can Do It

Field Day 3
Nonfiction

What a Climb 11
Fiction

HOUGHTON MIFFLIN   BOSTON

Printed in China

ISBN-13: 978-0-618-93249-8

ISBN-10: 0-618-93249-6

1 2 3 4 5 6 7 8 9 SDP 15 14 13 12 11 10 09 08

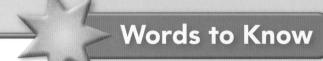

Words to Know

knee   climb

knots   thumbs

fair

Field Day

by Becky Manfredini

It is Field Day today. Do you know what happens at Field Day? Each child will play games, climb ropes, or run in races. We'll play fair and have lots of fun!

We'll have lots of races. Run as fast as you can! Try not to fall and scrape your knee.

Let's climb ropes. There are knots in the rope to help us hold on. We use our thumbs and all of our fingers to hold on!

Let's jump rope. First we jump slowly, and then we jump fast. Who can jump the longest?

We'll hop in a sack race, too. This is hard to do!

Let's play a game. We'll have
teams. There are lots of different
games we can play. Which outside
game do you like best?

It is time to go home. What a
fun day we had! I even got a prize.
Would you like to go to a Field Day?

8

Words to Know

knapsack   taught

knees   tight

knots   climb

know   crumb

sigh

gold   heavy

What a Climb

by Becky Manfredini

illustrated by Dan Grant

Kate and Ben will hike the trail.
They may climb the rocks, too.
It will be Kate's first climb. They
see a beautiful gold sunrise.

First, Ben packs a knapsack.
He fills it with snacks.
   Kate has a rope with knots.
They may need it to climb the rocks.

"Wow!" said Kate with a big sigh. "This trail is steep!"

Ben said, "I know this will be hard. We'll have fun, though!"

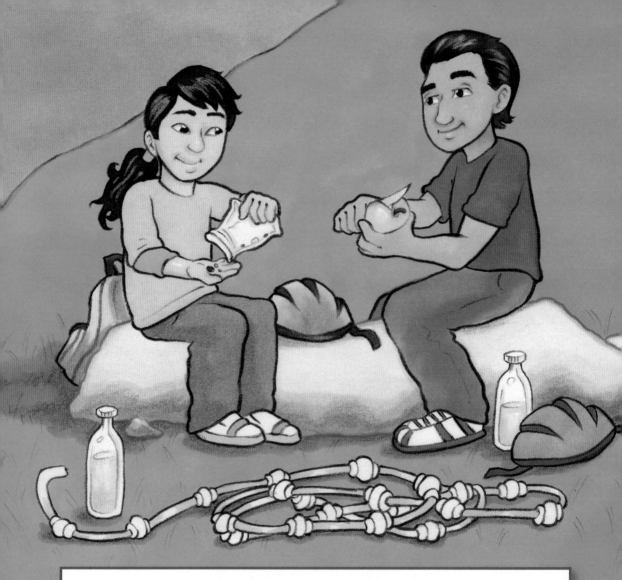

Ben and Kate climb for a while. The rope gets heavy. Kate's knees hurt.

"Let's have a snack," she said. She eats every crumb in the bag.

Kate and Ben stop at a pair of huge rocks.

"Let's climb these," said Ben.

He gets the rope and holds on tight. Kate will climb up next.

Then Kate and Ben climb down. Kate said, "I didn't think it was too hard. I'm glad you taught me how to climb."